Visiting a SALVATION ARMY CITADEL

Visiting a **SALVATION ARMY CITADEL**

Miriam Blackwell

Photography
MARK BROWN

Illustration/Design
JUDY BILLSON

LUTTERWORTH EDUCATIONAL
GUILDFORD, SURREY

The author wishes to thank the officers and corps at Tunbridge Wells Salvation Army Citadel for their help and co-operation in compiling this book. Special thanks are due to David Greenwood and Julia Dawson for their work on the plans and illustrations.

When you look up the passages from the Bible remember that the first number after the name of the book is the chapter number, and the other numbers refer to the verses; so, Mark 15:22–37 is Mark's Gospel, chapter 15, verses 22 to 37. If the verse numbers are written 22,37 it means verses 22 and 37.

First published in 1984

ISBN 0 7188 2572 1

Set in 11/12 point Univers by Nene Phototypesetters Ltd, Northampton
Printed and bound in Great Britain at The Camelot Press Ltd, Southampton

Contents

1.God's Marching Army

Imagine Tunbridge Wells on a sleepy Sunday morning. In a quiet street a man washes his car and two children play with a kitten. On the common dogs rummage among bracken for interesting scents while their owners wander idly across the grass. The sound of bells wafts over grey rooftops from the spire of St Peter's church. Suddenly another sound mingles with the chimes – a brass band playing a lively tune. The children run to look; the kitten scampers to the safety of his garden; the man swirls his car-cleaning cloth in time to the rhythmic beat of the band. Salvation Army soldiers are marching down the street!

AN OPEN-AIR MEETING

The **Salvationists**, as members of The Salvation Army are called, have come to hold an open-air meeting. They believe that the Christian message is so important that everyone should have the opportunity to hear it. This is why they hold meetings out of doors as well as in their **citadels** or halls. The Salvation Army is part of the Christian Church, a world-wide group of people who believe in Jesus Christ and try to follow his teaching as recorded in the Bible. This Army never fights against people but against wrong in the world. Its **soldiers** (another name for members) do all they can to help those in need because this is what Jesus did when he lived on earth. Many of them choose to wear **uniform** as a sign that they belong to God's Army.

The music in the street stops, but the tramp of feet continues as the Salvationists form a ring. Lace curtains twitch. People come to their windows, reluctant to be seen but happy to share the meeting from a distance.

The children settle on a wall to listen. Only the kitten ignores the bandmaster as he leads the singing:

'Come let us all unite to sing,
God is love!'

The yellow, red and blue flag tugs at its staff in the wind, revealing the motto of The Salvation Army woven into it. 'Blood and Fire' it reads, reminding Salvationists of the blood of Jesus who died for others, and the fire of the Holy Spirit which appeared in the room where the first disciples met at Whitsuntide. You can read about this in Acts, chapter 2, in the Bible.

The pictures show the progress of the meeting. Each Sunday meetings like this are held in hundreds of towns and villages throughout Britain so that people who never attend a church service can hear the **gospel** message. Gospel means good news. The main aim of Salvationists is to spread the good news that God loves all people, and this is one way to achieve that aim.

Many Salvation Army centres are in large cities where life can be difficult due to overcrowding and other conditions. They are surrounded by high rise flats or old, rundown houses. Salvationists there are involved in helping homeless people and caring for those whose lives are hard and drab.

Royal Tunbridge Wells does not have the same problems as an inner city area but behind the lace curtains in the large houses there are lonely people who need friends, children who need care, and many who are glad to know that Salvationists live and work in their town. Yes, there is plenty for the Army to do in Tunbridge Wells.

OUTSIDE THE CITADEL

When the open-air meeting is over the band leads the march back to the citadel, the building where they will join many others in a service of worship. Down the hill swings the procession, attracting attention as it passes, until it turns through white gates leading to the citadel, allowing traffic to flow freely again.

The forecourt of the citadel bustles with activity. A bright red minibus draws up in front of the porch. Elderly people climb carefully from the vehicle. They live in nearby Sunset Lodge, a residence for retired **officers**. These officers served for many years caring for other people. Now they in turn are being cared for but they have not retired from Christian living and they enjoy coming each week to worship God.

Outside the porch a chattering group surrounds a tiny baby held proudly by her mother. All the family has come to the meeting because it is a special occasion – the **dedication** of the baby. Everyone wants to share the happiness of her parents. You will find out more about this special ceremony on page 15.

Teenagers and children join the people moving towards the entrance as eleven o'clock approaches. Those of all ages are welcome at Salvation Army meetings. Young and old pause to watch the band come to a halt at the double beat of the drum. They all file into the hall to prepare for the **holiness** meeting. It is an important hour for every Salvationist: a time of learning and inspiration, with holy, or Christlike, living the theme of all that takes place.

2. Worship and witness

INSIDE THE CITADEL

A stranger might be surprised at the movement and murmuring inside the hall at first, but as eleven o'clock approaches everyone quietly takes a seat and prepares to worship God. While the congregation waits, the band plays softly.

Some Salvation Army halls are about a hundred years old but this is a modern one. Sunlight streams through a glass wall, reflecting from silvery instruments. It highlights the colourful flags and the crest standing out against the brick wall at the back of the platform where the songsters, or choir members, are seated. This platform, with a reading desk at the centre, takes the place at the front of the hall where an altar, pulpit and lectern would be in most churches.

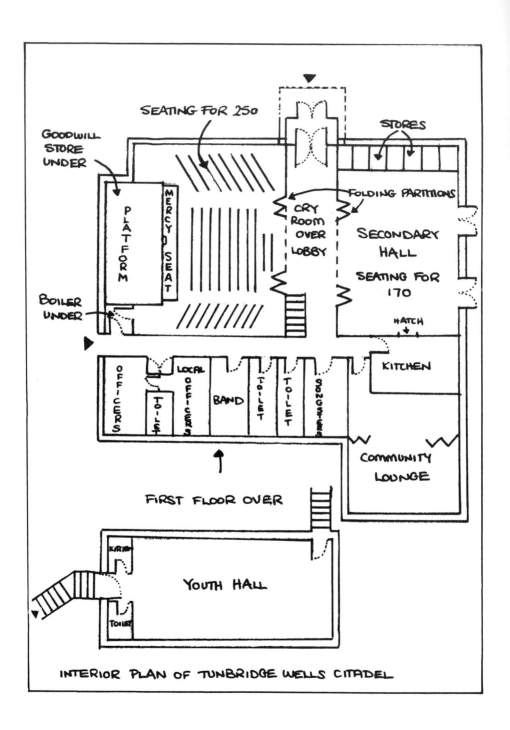

SEATING FOR 250

GOODWILL STORE UNDER

STORES

PLATFORM

MERCY SEAT

CRY ROOM OVER LOBBY

FOLDING PARTITIONS

SECONDARY HALL

SEATING FOR 170

BOILER UNDER

HATCH

OFFICERS

TOILET

LOCAL OFFICERS

BAND

TOILET

TOILET

SONGSTERS

KITCHEN

COMMUNITY LOUNGE

FIRST FLOOR OVER

KITCHEN

YOUTH HALL

TOILET

INTERIOR PLAN OF TUNBRIDGE WELLS CITADEL

A picture of Jesus hangs in front of the reading desk. Below this is an open Bible placed on the holiness table. These features remind the congregation that the preacher will pass on God's message to them.

Like all Salvation Army halls the building seems plain, with no elaborate decorations. The only other picture is a portrait of William Booth, the founder of the Army. Flowers are used to add colour and beauty.

THE MERCY SEAT

The mercy seat, or penitent form, is a long polished wooden bench in front of the platform. It is an important part of every Salvation Army citadel. There people can kneel if they feel the need to ask God for his help and guidance, to seek his forgiveness if they have done wrong, or to make special promises. Many make their first decision to follow Jesus and live a Christian life, kneeling here. This experience is called conversion. Salvationists believe that, while people can be near to God in any place, it is helpful to share such important moments with friends who will encourage them.

During most meetings a special time of prayer is set aside when people are invited to kneel at the mercy seat. Sometimes a person might feel moved to go forward at other times. An experienced Christian counsels any people seeking help and prays with them there.

Apart from this unique feature, the rest of the body of the hall is filled with rows of chairs. More can be added by removing partitions which form the back wall, thus including the lobby and smaller hall.

THE YOUNG PEOPLE'S HALL

The second hall is used mainly for children's meetings but many other activities take place there too. A hatch at the side, leading to a kitchen, shows that meals are served here. There are large cupboards for storing equipment, and boards for charts and notices. You can see from the plan that there are many smaller rooms which are well used by various groups of people. Although the hall was only recently built plans have already been made to add more space. An extra hall has been built above the side rooms for active groups like youth and children's clubs.

THE HOLINESS MEETING

Each Sunday morning the rows of seats in the senior hall are almost full. Tiny babies on their mothers' laps, elderly people who have been part of this corps or group for many years, and friends of all ages feel at home here. They know that they share the privilege of worship and service with Christians in all parts of the world.

From a door at the side of the platform the commanding officers enter to lead the worship. As this title suggests, they are the people in charge of the corps. Their busy life is described in chapter 3. In this corps the commanding officers are majors. Elsewhere they might be lieutenants or captains. Sometimes one person commands a corps.

Soon everyone is praising God; the band and the congregation blending in the joyful music of the opening song. Salvationists

enjoy singing, but they value too the quiet moments of prayer which follow. Any member of the congregation is invited to speak to God aloud, on behalf of others.

No one, except the leader, knows exactly what will happen because Salvation Army meetings do not follow a set pattern. The Major has prepared carefully, trying to include something that everyone, young and old, will find helpful. Because Salvation Army beliefs are based on the Bible, he has chosen a passage from this important book. It is read aloud, clearly and slowly, so that people can follow the words in their own Bibles. Later he gives a sermon, or talk, to explain the ideas in the passage. The Major's wife, who is also a trained officer, takes her turn at leading the meeting and preaching.

An unusual feature of Salvation Army worship is **testimony** time. The commanding officers are not the only ones to speak in a meeting. Sometimes they invite others to talk about experiences of life as a Christian. This is called **giving a testimony**.

THE BABY'S DEDICATION

Now comes the part of the meeting which one family in the congregation will always remember — the baby's dedication. Her mother carries the baby to the platform and her father follows, leading his other small daughter by the hand. The Major takes the baby in his arms, hoping that she will not cry. He reads out loud the promises the parents are about to make to bring up the child according to Christian teaching and Salvation Army principles. They realize that it is a big responsibility to care for a new life, and join in the prayer that God will help them in their task. A colourful certificate is handed to them to remind them of this important occasion.

THE SERMON

Not every holiness meeting includes a dedication but most of them have a sermon. This is the time when the congregation is taught about God and the Christian life. The small children who have tried to sit still for a long time often begin to fidget so they leave the grown ups and go into the young people's hall. In the more relaxed surroundings they have their own activities and learn about God in a way they understand and enjoy. Some Army halls have a special 'cry room' with a large window looking into the hall so that adults can look after small children and still follow the meeting themselves.

The officer has prepared his talk carefully, believing that it is God's message to his people. They will be challenged to think about their progress as members of God's Army. Some may kneel at the mercy seat to make an important decision to follow Jesus Christ more faithfully. Finally the Major prays that God will help everyone present to understand the message and be useful, joyful Christians in the coming days. After a few quiet moments the organ plays as the people leave the hall.

THE SUNDAY PROGRAMME

Most Salvation Army corps have a full programme each Sunday. Once a month at Tunbridge Wells an afternoon **praise meeting**, described in chapter 4, follows the children's company meeting (Sunday school). Sometimes there is an open-air meeting after tea. This is followed by another regular service, the **Salvation**

meeting. Salvationists hope that people who do not belong to the Army will accept invitations to this meeting so that they can learn more about God and his Kingdom.

After the evening meeting the teenagers are still ready for more! Sometimes they meet informally at someone's home for coffee and a chat. Tomorrow, at work or school, they will try to put into practice the things they have learnt at the Army about being a Christian.

Other corps have similar programmes with some variations in details. Changes are made in order to make best use of the time. For instance, in a holiday resort, a corps might hold an open-air meeting after the Salvation meeting. People often take an evening stroll and have time to stop and listen to the gospel message.

Salvationists feel that meeting for worship is an essential part of a Christian's life. Just as a car needs to be filled with petrol before it can make a journey, people who try to serve God find renewed strength by joining with others in praise and prayer. Their day of worship and witness prepares them for the week ahead.

3. Appointed to lead

An army fights best when it has good leaders who organize the battle efficiently and encourage the soldiers. The Salvation Army has thousands of men and women who take the responsibility of becoming leaders, or officers, to use the military term.

COMMISSIONED OFFICERS

You have already met the Major and his officer-wife. They are in charge of a corps and have a similar role to that of a minister or a priest in another church. They are both commissioned officers. Commissioned officers are men and women who have left their original job and taken a course of training. This prepares them to work full time in The Salvation Army. Both men and women have

this opportunity because William Booth felt that every willing, capable worker should be accepted for service in the Army.

The Major has been a Salvationist all his life. He likes to tell people about how he came to be an officer:

'I lived in Bristol when I was a boy. My mum and dad were in the Army and I used to go along to the corps with them. At school my favourite subject was science and I did well enough to qualify as a chemist after I left school.

My first job was with the Gas Board where I put my knowledge to good use. Although I loved this work I had a growing feeling that I should work full time in the Army. I read in the Bible about Simon Peter and Andrew who left their jobs as fishermen to work with Jesus (you can find the story in Mark 1:16–18). It took some courage when I decided to follow their example and give all my time as an officer in God's Army.'

TRAINING TO BE AN OFFICER

Some months after this decision the Major went to The Salvation Army's **International Training College** in London to be a **cadet**. There he had very little spare time. He attended classes in Bible study and many other subjects which would prepare him for his future as an officer. Part of the time was spent away from college at a corps where the commanding officer gave him lots of practical advice.

WOMEN OFFICERS

The Major had already met the girl who was to become his wife. He was happy that she too wanted to be an officer. When she was only eight she heard someone talking about his work as an officer in the Army overseas. It sounded so thrilling that she made up her mind there and then that she would train to be an officer when she was old enough!

Many Salvation Army officers are women. William Booth's wife, Catherine, was not content with being a busy wife and mother like most Victorian women. She felt that she must be active in the 'war'

which the Army fights, and other women were glad to follow her example. William Booth once said that his best soldiers were women! He had proved that women were capable of sharing work with men. Often they became leaders. Evangeline Booth, one of his daughters, became the **General**, the international leader of the Army.

It is a Salvation Army rule that if an officer wants to marry, he or she must choose another officer or a person who intends to become an officer, as a partner. This may seem a strict rule to you, but it is a sensible one. When two people have the same aims and ideals they are more likely to work happily in partnership. Some people resign from officership to marry partners who are not officers, but still serve God as soldiers in the Army. A soldier may marry a person who is not a Salvationist but many in fact choose a partner who finds joy in sharing Christian service.

COMMISSIONING DAY

At the end of a two year course at the Army's training college, cadets attend a memorable **commissioning ceremony**. Friends

and relatives join them to celebrate the beginning of their lives as officers. There are solemn moments when the cadets promise to be loyal to God. There are moments of surprise when they receive their appointments and learn where they will live and work. Many of them will be sent to take charge of a corps somewhere in the United Kingdom, or to help other, experienced officers. Some will go to Salvation Army social service centres – a **hostel** for homeless people, a children's home or an eventide home for the elderly. Some may be sent overseas to work in hospitals or schools. The continuing growth of the Salvation Army depends on these young people who answer God's call to service. There is great rejoicing when new reinforcements are commissioned.

Many years ago the Major was commissioned to a small corps in London. He was then a **lieutenant**, which is the first rank of a Salvation Army officer. Two years later he married, when his wife had completed her own training at the college.

AN ARMY WEDDING

Theirs was a typical Army wedding. The bride and groom wore their Salvation Army uniforms and the flag was held beside them to remind them that their partnership would help them to work for God more effectively. The wedding ceremony itself was very similar to the one used in other Christian churches. Flowers and music added to the festive occasion. At an Army wedding the couple exchange rings and, as well as promising to be faithful to each other, they declare that their marriage will not prevent them from obediently serving God.

Salvation Army weddings are not, on the whole, elaborate, expensive celebrations but they do not lack in enjoyment. Because Salvationists do not drink alcohol the usual toasts to the bride and groom, if included, are drunk in fruit juice. This does not prevent everyone from warmly wishing them every happiness in their life together.

A COMMANDING OFFICER'S RESPONSIBILITIES

The Major and his officer-wife have to be prepared to serve at any time of the day or night. They not only lead worship on Sundays, organize daily activities, deal with corps finance and property and care for their soldiers; other people in the community claim attention too. No one is turned away because he is not a Salvationist. Jesus taught that if someone does something to help any needy person he is serving God. You can read his words in the Bible in Matthew 25:40. The Majors try to remember this.

Sunday is the most important day in the officers' week. They faithfully teach God's word, as told in the Bible, both at the citadel and out of doors. In this way they hope to help people to understand the Christian way of life. During the week they spend time in study and thought to prepare for the meetings. They believe that they must honour God first and then all other activities will have purpose.

SALVATION ARMY PAPERS

Each week the Army publishes a religious paper called **The War Cry**. Officers and soldiers take it to places where people gather, like public houses, so that as many as possible have the chance to buy one. Often customers are glad to talk to Salvationists about the Christian faith. Some people like to buy **The Young Soldier** for their children. This weekly paper has been on sale for more than a hundred years. In it there are puzzles, jokes, letters from children, interesting articles and always a story from the Bible. Salvationists enjoy reading **The Musician** which keeps them informed about corps activities. There are magazines about other Army work too, and books by Salvation Army authors. The corps officers value this means of spreading the gospel.

LOCAL OFFICERS

The commanding officers could not possibly lead every activity held at the corps but they like to attend as many as possible to encourage the **local officers**. These are volunteer workers who do the kind of jobs which occur in most churches – treasurer, hall keeper, secretary and so on. Some are given military titles as you would expect in an army. The **sergeant-major** holds an important office and you can probably guess what the **welcome sergeant** does.

A small group of local officers forms the census board. They meet regularly to revise the list, or roll, of soldiers of a corps. They add the names of new soldiers. Adults may join the movement at any age but most soldiers are enrolled in their late teens. If Salvationists no longer wish to be soldiers, their names can be removed from the roll. This is only done after much thought and consultation with a senior officer. Should anyone break an important rule, then membership might be suspended for a while but this only happens in extreme cases.

Another important group, the **corps council**, meets to discuss plans and talk about the work of the corps. People of all ages, representing every aspect of corps life, join the census board to form this council. Not only do they talk about plans; they work hard to put them into practice too.

WEEKLY ACTIVITIES

Like most churches the Army has a weekly meeting especially for women. This is called the **home league**. If you look at the picture of the badge you will see that it shows a house standing on a book.

The aim of the home league is to show the importance of basing family life on the teaching of Jesus. The book represents the Bible.

The **home league secretary** and her assistants are responsible for all this activity but the officers like to spend some time with the members too. In the same way they show interest in the Over 60 club, the **Man Alive group**, band and songster practices and all the children's activities you can read about in chapter 7. Salvationists meet for prayer and worship during the week as well.

VISITS

Visiting people in their homes is an important part of an officer's work. Housebound people, mostly the elderly and sick, can easily become isolated. They are glad to hear news about the corps to keep them in touch. The Major and his officer-wife try to make sure that they are well cared for and give practical help where it is needed. They read verses from the Bible and pray so that the housebound person knows that he is still part of God's family although unable to worship at the Army citadel. Active soldiers are

visited too, so that the officers can get to know them in an informal, personal way. Understanding each other helps people to work happily together.

THE LARGER CHRISTIAN FAMILY

The Salvation Army officers like to meet other Christian leaders in Tunbridge Wells as in many other places. They regularly meet at ecumenical gatherings which are meetings of ministers and priests from different local churches. They exchange news and discuss ways in which they can work together in the town. Many years ago Salvationists were not always invited to ecumenical events. Some church leaders thought that The Salvation Army was not a true church. Their main criticism was that the Army did not observe important ceremonies like holy communion. Salvationists believe that they can come near to God without actually receiving bread and wine as a symbol of God's presence. They do not believe that it is wrong to take part in such acts and are not forbidden to do so, if invited to share by fellow Christians from another church. Gradually understanding has increased and most Christian groups are happy to recognize the Army, its women as well as its men officers, and its distinctive style of worship.

The Major and his officer-wife are leaders in the 'Army of the Helping Hand', as The Salvation Army has been called, and so they know that each day will be very busy. Unexpected calls have to be fitted into an already full programme. The phone can ring in the early hours of the morning, bringing news of a difficult problem needing urgent attention; their car, loaded with old clothes for the jumble sale, can break down. But their despair changes to hope quite soon. They remember that God has given them strength and guidance for many years and they work on together faithfully.

Throughout Britain and in more than eighty other countries men and women Salvation Army officers are working in corps, some of them alone, leading groups of soldiers in the fight against wrong. They realize that they are responsible not only to their General, but to God.

4. With trumpet and voice

Music has been used to praise God since very early times. The Psalmist wrote:

'Praise him with the sound of the trumpet!'

If you read Psalm 150 in the Bible you will see that other instruments were used in worship too.

EARLY ARMY MUSIC

Since the Army was founded more than a hundred years ago, most of these instruments, and others, have been used by Salvationists. Perhaps not a psaltery, a very ancient instrument, but equally strange ones like melodeons and tin whistles were once pressed into service. Brass instruments proved to be the best. They have a clear, bright sound and can be carried easily for use in open-air meetings and marches. Now most Salvation Army corps have

brass bands. There may be just a few players or a full band of more than thirty people. Whatever the size it plays to honour God.

The Tunbridge Wells corps has had a band for many years. In a magazine dated 1907 there is a list of thirty-one bandsmen. There was Mr Allison, the solo cornet player, a master bootmaker by trade. His daughter-in-law still sings in the **songster brigade**, or choir, today. There was also a cutler and tinker, a bacon dryer and a page boy among the bandsmen! The drummer had been a poacher before he joined the Army. Another was described as 'a very wild lad' who tormented the band at Brighton until he discovered that there was a better way of life, and became a member of the Army he once opposed.

A photograph shows that they were smartly dressed in military style uniforms. Bandsmen knew that they should honour God by their good behaviour as well as by their smart appearance and tuneful playing. These early bandsmen set a fine example and some of their children and grandchildren still serve in the corps.

THE BAND TODAY

Today's band is just as efficient. Each member is a Christian and has been **enrolled** or **sworn in** as a Salvation Army soldier in a simple ceremony. You can read more about this in chapter 7. They have also promised to be loyal bandsmen or women, remembering that they are not just members of a performing band but Christian soldiers whose music must be used to spread the gospel message.

All the members of the band are volunteers and are not paid for their service. Like the early bandsmen, they have ordinary jobs and fit Salvation Army activities into their free time. Some of the music played by the band is quite difficult and needs careful practice. All of it is written or arranged specially for Army bands to play.

On a typical Sunday afternoon the citadel is a hive of activity as the band prepares to take part in a praise meeting. In the young people's hall the company meeting is just finishing.

'Please leave quietly,' requests the **young people's sergeant major**, 'and be careful not to push our visitors over in your hurry!'

Visitors? There must be some important people around.

A MUSICAL FESTIVAL

The important people are gathering in the big hall. Some have arrived by coach or minibus, some in cars and some even by wheel-chair. They are all elderly or handicapped and have been specially invited to share an afternoon of praise in music and song. For some it is a rare treat to leave home at all. To enjoy the Salvationists' bright music and good company makes it a specially happy occasion. After the **festival** of music they will have tea and cakes before returning home.

The festival progresses and it is the turn of the songsters. Their song is based on words from the Bible:

> 'Fear thou not, for I am with thee, be not afraid for I am thy God!'

Some of the visitors are blind and are often lonely and afraid. Perhaps they will remember these words in the coming days and will be courageous.

Each songster, like the bandsmen, is a Salvation Army soldier. The brigade sings Christian songs of many kinds, most of them written by Salvationists. Some are lively and joyful; others are quiet prayers to God. They meet each week for practice and most of them attend other activities at the citadel. Sometimes songster brigades go to other churches to share worship. They also visit prisons, hospitals, and other places where people welcome a change from dull routine.

TIMBREL GROUP

'What did you like best?' you might ask the visitors at the end of the musical festival, and many would reply, 'The timbrel'. Timbrel is another name for the tambourine, a small percussion instrument with metal jingles round a drum head. The girls in the group make a series of movements in time to music, using the tambourine.

Praise meetings like this are held at all Salvation Army corps. If it is a special occasion a musical group from another corps might be invited to share the festival. Sometimes one purpose of the event is to raise money. The collection from this festival at Tunbridge Wells was given to the president of the local association for the blind. They were very pleased to add £75 to their funds.

MUSICAL DRAMA

Drama is another way in which Salvationists worship God. The Tunbridge Wells corps produced a musical version of the story of Hosea, a character in the Old Testament of the Bible. *Hosea* is just one of the many musicals which Salvationists have produced in recent years.

Salvationists find their music a useful way of serving God. It helps them to spread the gospel message, it cheers and comforts those who hear, and it brings joy to those who work together to produce a good sound. No wonder the founder, **William Booth**, said,

'Sing so as to make the world hear.'

5. At your service

Ask many people what they know about The Salvation Army and they will say vaguely,

'Oh they help people . . .'

In Tunbridge Wells the title of 'The Army of the helping hand' is well deserved.

Every member of the corps is involved in this caring ministry in some way. Some spend many hours in active **goodwill** community service, meeting needs of the elderly or underprivileged in practical ways. Others help by giving money or making things to sell. All of them work as a team under the leadership of the **secretary**.

Naturally he is a very busy man. If he had time to write a diary a typical entry for a week might read:

Monday:

Visited the hospital with some **league of mercy** members. The medical social worker said how grateful she is for the

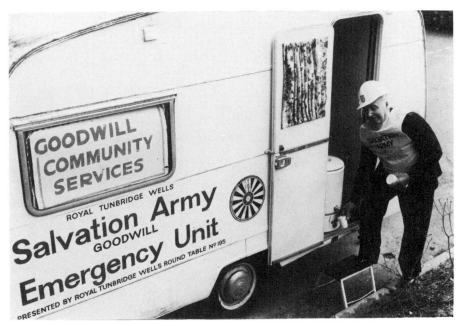

help of reliable people who visit those who have no family in town. Helped one lady to write a letter to The Salvation Army **Investigation Department**. Her son lives in New Zealand and she has lost touch with him. The Department traces many missing relatives. They will contact Salvationists in New Zealand and seek their help. Mrs May would dearly love a letter from her son.

Sent some blankets to Oxfam. Must remember to thank members of the knitting group who spent so much time unpicking the woollen garments and knitting squares. These blankets are light and warm. Very welcome in emergencies.

Tuesday:

Phone call from the police – could we help families whose homes have been flooded? River Medway burst banks after heavy rainfall. Took emergency vehicle. Supplied hot drinks and food to families and firemen who were busy pumping out the muddy water. Several houses under two feet of water.

Later took second-hand armchairs from our store to replace those ruined by water – also bed for elderly lady in bungalow. Her mattress is so muddy it isn't fit to use again. Contacted bandsmen to come this evening to help clean up. Women from corps will help tomorrow. The officer's wife stayed to comfort old lady and assure her she is safe.

Wednesday:

Shopping at cash and carry store to replace stocks of food. Day centre – 60 for hot lunch at hall: roast beef and potatoes, sprouts, Yorkshire pudding; chocolate sponge and sauce. All lonely people. Some handicapped. Must arrange for someone to call on Mrs Jones who hasn't been for two weeks. Can accept two people from waiting list because Mr and Mrs Oak are moving away. A good crowd at the over-60 club. Day centre folk enjoyed the company.

Talked to Joanne, a teenager who arrived at the hall very upset. Said her mum doesn't want her. She calmed down after a while and agreed to let someone go and talk to her family. Hope to make things happier there. Will invite Joanne to the **youth club**.

Thursday:

Did some gardening at home. Don't know how I found time for everything before I retired from business!

Made poster to remind everyone about the 'Share your bread' lunch on Sunday week. Must remember to order the rolls from the baker. Hope to raise a good sum of money for the Army's feeding programme at the **Shelter for the destitute** in Sri Lanka. It's staggering to think how many can be fed with the money we would normally spend on one Sunday lunch. The picture on the poster should remind us to share willingly.

Friday:

Trip to London in the van. Took good supply of used clothing for people at Salvation Army centres there. First call, Blackfriars hostel for men. Captain there said everyone is thrilled with the new freezer our Christmas gift money bought. There was enough left to buy an organ for the meeting room where the residents and staff worship. Made arrangements for fifty of the men to come to Tunbridge

35

Wells next month for a coach outing with dinner at the hall and a picnic tea in the country. These otherwise homeless men really enjoy a day away from the dust and noise of the city. They are very excited about it.

Saturday

An early start. The minibus full of noisy children headed for the coast. Most children these days have outings to the sea but these are from homes where things are difficult. Dad away. Mum not well. No spare money for holidays. What joy to see them leaping down the beach – stopping suddenly when they felt the cold waves! It was quieter coming home – all worn out. Thanked God for fine weather and safe journeys.

Sunday:

Managed to wake in time to be at the hall early. Always someone to welcome. Called at Mr Wright's after meeting. His wife died this week. He'll be very lonely now. Tried to show him we care and will help all we can. Must remember to keep an eye on him. Perhaps he will come to the day centre after a week or two. Major called to make arrangements for the funeral service.

Good to see members of the over-60 club at the meeting for the first time. Said they enjoyed worshipping with us and would come again.

We enjoyed the day's meetings too. Talked about all the events of the week while we had our evening coffee. We are grateful to God for so many opportunities to serve other people – and for strength to do it!

What a busy week. Perhaps not every week is quite so hectic for the secretary of the goodwill league and his members but there is plenty to keep them busy.

CHRISTMAS JOY

Christmas time always calls for extra effort. Gifts, sweets, toys are taken to those glad to be remembered at this time. Each of the men at Blackfriars hostel receives a carefully wrapped parcel on Christmas morning. They really feel part of the Tunbridge Wells family.

THE PLAYGROUP

Salvationists know of families where there is not much money to spare for treats. They invite the children to a Christmas party and the excitement soon spreads. However, some of the tiny children seem to be afraid of meeting strangers, so members of the corps organize a regular playgroup where the children can make friends and learn to play together happily. Every week they meet in a sunny room at the citadel. They are collected by car or minibus and their mothers enjoy a chance to catch up with the housework or the shopping in peace. Now they too feel they are part of the Army family.

MONEY RAISING

Salvationists find that if people know about the work being done to help those in need they will give generously. Plans are now being made to build an extension for a comfortable day centre for the elderly. This is possible because a lady donated her house to the Army when she died.

So the caring work for the community goes on quietly, day by day. Wherever there are Salvationists such help is available to anyone in need.

6. Veterans remember

On a fine Sunday you might see a group of elderly men and women resting on a bench outside the citadel, waiting to go inside when it is time for the meeting. If you could listen to their conversation you would learn a great deal about the exciting early days of The Salvation Army.

'What a good thing we have a large car park,' says one. 'Nearly everyone arrives by car these days. I remember when we walked three miles to the hall from where we lived at Rusthall. Only very wealthy people had cars when we were small. Just think – it's seventy years ago!'

THE FIRST SUNDAY SCHOOL OUTINGS

They remember the outings to Hastings in the great steam trains, and the picnics on the common arranged by their teachers.

As their thoughts run on they remember hearing about the day the General, William Booth, came to town, just before they were born. By this time, in 1905, the people of Tunbridge Wells respected the Army and thousands crowded the streets to greet the General. The Army had not always been so popular as you will see.

THE EAST LONDON CHRISTIAN MISSION

The Salvation Army began in the East End of London in 1865. At this time it was called the **East London Christian Mission**. William Booth and his wife Catherine did all they could to tell people the good news of Jesus Christ. Poverty surrounded them. They organized cheap food shops and hostels for the homeless. Gradually the movement grew because many who heard William preach became Christians and wanted to help the work among needy people.

THE SALVATION ARMY

In 1878 a new idea came to them. Why not call the Mission an **Army**? Those who joined had to fight against wrong. It could be 'The Salvation Army', whose soldiers were saved from the unhappiness of a sinful life. So the Army marched out into the streets with bands and banners. Now no one could ignore them and their war against evil.

CATHERINE BOOTH VISITS TUNBRIDGE WELLS

Catherine was a great preacher. It was unusual in those days for a woman to speak in public and she always drew a crowd. Catherine led the way for many women who have been able to serve God actively in The Salvation Army.

During her preaching tours Catherine Booth met many people who became supporters of the new movement. In Tunbridge Wells she met Mr and Mrs Reed. They lived in a large house with beautiful grounds called 'Dunorlan'. Now the grounds are a public park not far from the citadel. The Reeds were good, generous people. Not only did they give money towards a large hall in Whitechapel, London, but they also paid for many of the poor city

dwellers to spend a day at their country home. Mrs Booth conducted meetings in the Assembly Room on the Pantiles. Here a small mission had been opened, encouraged by Mr Reed. It was not very successful however, and when the Reeds went away to Australia the mission soon closed.

TINKER LANE AT TUNBRIDGE WELLS

At that point another important character entered our story – Tinker Lane. He travelled around Kent selling and mending pots and pans. At any opportunity he preached about God because he was a keen Christian. During his travels he heard about The Salvation Army. 'Just the thing for Tunbridge Wells,' he thought.

After a search he found a hall that could be used. The rent was low because of the filthy state of the hall, so Tinker Lane scrubbed and scraped until it was fit to use. He begged wood for a platform and benches from a local saw mill and then wrote to Bramwell Booth, William's son and assistant, asking for a leader.

A young Salvation Army officer, Charlotte Bateson, was sent to **open fire** and start the work in the town. It was not easy. Many people disliked the noisy, enthusiastic Christians. They thought that worship should be quiet and dignified – but the Salvationists wanted to shout and sing for joy! After all some of them had been saved from a life of crime and misery. The owner of the hall said they must leave because they were causing so much trouble.

THE SKELETON ARMY

For a while nobody else would let the group hire a hall. This was difficult but the Salvationists did not give up. They used any building they could find. Sometimes for months at a time they had to hold all their meetings in the open-air. Then the skeleton army went into action!

Every time Salvationists marched in the streets or held a meeting on the common, a gang of ruffians tried to stop them. Some people who wanted the Army to leave the town persuaded these thugs to attack with sticks and stones. One day they drenched some Salvationists with stinking fish water! The best method to overcome this problem was to win the opposition for God. Some of the worst ruffians became dramatically changed when they stopped to listen to the message and realized that the good news of God's love was for them too.

At last a new hall was built in Varney Street and everyone rejoiced. The Salvationists had proved that they were in the town to stay. Gradually they won the respect and understanding of the townspeople who saw the good work being done in the community.

THE FOUNDER'S VISIT

It was a great day in 1905, when William Booth entered the town in a new-fangled motor car he had borrowed. Crowds came to cheer him; brass instruments shone in the sun; flags fluttered joyfully and everyone fell silent when the Founder spoke words of encouragement:

> 'Hallelujah!' echoed the Salvationists.
> 'God bless the General.'

The friends on the bench smile when they think of those days long ago, and later times, when they were young and active in the corps. They agree that there were good experiences in the past, but they look forward too. They have confidence that the young people in the corps today will continue working for God in the years ahead.

7. Tomorrow's Army

When you have read this chapter I think you will agree that 'tomorrow's Army' will not be a disappointment. Some of the young people in the corps belong to Army families and have always been involved in the movement. Others knew nothing about the Army until they were invited by a friend, or joined one of the activities. Susan doesn't remember the first time she went to the Army with her Salvationist parents because it was when she was only two weeks old, fourteen years ago.

THE PRIMARY

When she was three she was old enough to join the **primary**. This is a class for children aged between three and seven years which is

held in most corps. The children love to sing choruses about Jesus and hear stories from the Bible. The **primary sergeant** leads the group. She shows colourful pictures or perhaps uses puppets or paper figures to make the stories come to life. The children draw, make models and sometimes act the story themselves. Salvationists believe that it is good if children can learn about God when they are small even though they may not understand everything they hear.

THE JUNIOR MEETING

Primary members look forward to the day when they can join the 'big school' as they sometimes call the **junior meetings**. At Tunbridge Wells the children from the age of seven meet together twice on a Sunday but in some corps there is only one junior meeting. The children sing, pray and learn about the Bible and Salvation Army beliefs which are called **Doctrines**. At this time Susan began to understand more about being a Christian. Her parents guided and helped her when she was young but they hoped that, as she grew older, she would make her own promise to work for God. Thoughtfully she decided that she wanted to follow the example of Jesus, loving and serving others. She asked if she could become a junior soldier.

JUNIOR SOLDIERS

Susan was enrolled in a short ceremony during a meeting at the citadel. Many boys and girls between the ages of seven and fourteen become junior soldiers, signing a card to confirm their promise. They believe that God will help them to keep his laws, and they promise to pray and to read the Bible so their knowledge of God will grow.

In many corps the junior soldiers work at an **Award Scheme**. Their leader, the **junior soldier sergeant**, organizes all the work they do to earn badges. The first badge is the bronze award. Each

junior soldier has to pass eight sections before earning it. These are the sections:

Compulsory

Bible reader
Prayer writer
Army knowledge
Helper

Choice of four from:

Artist
Diarist
Who's who
Musician

Reciter
Punctuality
Recruiter
Scrap book

Susan's mother was pleased when she did the helper section. She had to sign a card each time Susan did a helpful task. By the time juniors have completed the bronze, silver and gold awards they are experienced young Salvationists.

THE SINGING COMPANY

Junior soldiers may become members of the **singing company**. Susan enjoys singing and she attends the weekly practice at the hall. The group takes part in the meetings and sometimes,

especially at Christmas, sings to elderly and sick people in homes and hospitals. Several of the girls play in the timbrel group mentioned in chapter 4.

THE YOUNG PEOPLE'S BAND

The young people's band is also composed of junior soldiers, both boys and girls. It is not easy to play a brass instrument. Many of the children begin to learn when they are seven or eight years old. Members of the senior band give time to teach them. They know they must practise regularly if they want to be skilled enough to play in the band.

THE CORPS CADET BRIGADE

When young Salvationists wish to have further serious training they join the **corps cadet brigade**. This group of young people under the leadership of the corps cadet **guardian** plays an active part in the corps. Susan joined the brigade when she was twelve years old. In it she had the opportunity of studying the Bible in more depth and discussing Army beliefs and activities. Corps cadets hold open-air meetings, sell Salvation Army newspapers, visit the sick and lonely and in fact assist the commanding officer as much as possible. Each corps cadet takes a correspondence course of Bible study which helps him or her to become a mature Christian.

OTHER ACTIVITIES

Boys and girls who are not junior soldiers can take part in other activities. Most corps have some kind of youth club. Many have Guide and Scout groups. There are Guides and Brownie Guides at Tunbridge Wells and the boys can join **SABAC** – the Salvation Army Boys' Adventure Corps. Peter is a member of SABAC. Unlike Susan he had no link with the Army or any other church when he was small. One of his school friends invited him to SABAC, and Peter certainly found it more adventurous than watching television at home.

Before long, Peter went to the Army on Sundays as well. He had never thought much about God, but now he realized that life was much more exciting for Christians than he had imagined. You might think that he would feel out of place among the Salvationists, but all are welcome at the Army whether they have belonged all their life or never had any connection before. Some months later Peter became a junior soldier and was proud to join this Army which had been unknown to him until his friend's introduction.

TRANSFER TO THE SENIOR CORPS

Susan and Peter will soon leave the young people's corps. At the age of fourteen they will be given the opportunity to become senior soldiers. All the training they have received has prepared them for this step but there are many things to consider carefully before being sworn in as senior soldiers. Salvationists, who can join at any age over fourteen, sign the **Articles of War** when they become full members of the Army. This is a document which sets

out in detail the beliefs of Salvationists and the promises they intend to make.

Other Christians share the beliefs of The Salvation Army but some of the promises are not so common. For instance Salvationists promise not to drink alcohol or smoke. One reason for this is that both alcohol and tobacco are harmful to health. They are very expensive too. William Booth and his workers saw many whose lives had been destroyed by excessive drinking. Booth realized that when some of these people became converted to God's way they would find it difficult to overcome their desire for alcohol, and so he felt that it would be helpful if Salvationists set an example by drinking only non-alcoholic drinks. Today there are still many problems in the world caused by excessive drinking of alcohol and so Salvationists consider it wise to continue to keep the Founder's pledge.

So Peter and Susan will solemnly stand beside the Army flag and sign the Articles of War at their swearing-in ceremony. The congregation of soldiers and friends will share this special occasion, glad to welcome two more loyal soldiers and friends of Christ into their corps and the world-wide Salvation Army.

THE BROADER VIEW

The Salvation Army at Tunbridge Wells is representative of more than eight hundred corps in Britain. Each corps has a similar programme, varying according to its size and location. Many Salvationists are involved in social service and goodwill community work in a chain of activity which spreads around the world in more than eighty countries.

Just as the Major left his home corps at Bristol as a young man, many have left Tunbridge Wells to serve in other places. You remember about Tinker Lane who appeared in chapter 6? His daughter is now a retired officer who has given a lifetime of adventurous Christian service in the Army. She spent many years in the Caribbean working in homes for teenage girls. Other young people have gone to the Army training college and are now serving in different parts of England, in corps and social centres.

It would take a very large book to write about all those who think of Tunbridge Wells as their Christian home. Just as ripples spread outwards from a stone dropped in a lake, so the influence of soldiers and officers who have worked faithfully in the corps year by year has spread further than they would imagine.

8. Over to you

The trouble with learning about new things is that we often discover how little we really know! You will have learnt a great deal about The Salvation Army if you have read this book, but you will probably realize that a study of a movement with more than a hundred years of history and work in over eighty countries is an unending project.

To make your study come to life try to contact a Salvation Army centre and speak to people who are Salvationists. There may be a Salvation Army soldier living in your district. You will find out if there is a corps near your home by looking in the telephone directory under 'Salvation Army'. The corps officers' home address is given and they would be pleased to hear from you if you are seriously interested in discovering more. Other kinds of centres are listed too. Although officers are very busy they will try to make time to tell you about their work.

Remember that anyone is welcome to attend a meeting at any citadel. Look out for open-air meetings too, and talk to one of the soldiers about your project. Always have a note book handy. Jot down briefly things you discover before you forget them. When your research is nearly complete organize the facts under suitable headings before writing them neatly in sentences on good paper. Careful drawings and photographs add interest to your study which should be as personal as possible. Your own observations, criticisms and thoughts will add value to the project. Resist the temptation to copy passages from books. This would spoil the unique quality of your work.

A tape recorder could be used to record music, sound effects and interviews. Make sure you have a number of questions in mind (or on paper) before you begin a conversation with a Salvationist. Talk until you are both confident before you switch on the microphone. Don't forget to play it back before you leave in case there is a technical hitch!

If history interests you, you would enjoy a visit to the small museum at Nottingham, in the house where William Booth was born, or the one in the Army shop in London. The addresses are:

> William Booth Memorial Complex,
> 12 Notintone Place,
> Sneinton Road, Nottingham NG2 4OG

> Salvationist Publishing & Supplies Ltd,
> 117–121 Judd Street,
> King's Cross, London WC1H 9NN

Packs of information leaflets and pictures are available if you write to:

> The Schools' Information Service,
> International Headquarters,
> 101 Queen Victoria Street, London EC4P 4EP

This service is glad to help students and teachers by arranging visiting speakers. Films and slides are also available.

A booklet called 'This Army Offers You . . .' can be obtained from this address too. It lists opportunities for Christians to work in the Army in many spheres in a voluntary or paid capacity.

So now it's over to you! Try to find out more about the adventure of Christian service in The Salvation Army.

Book List

Church buildings

P. J. Hunt, *Churches and Chapels*, Watts
P. J. Hunt, *What to look for inside a church*, Ladybird
P. J. Hunt, *What to look for outside a church*, Ladybird

About the Salvation Army

Cyril Barnes, *Army without Guns*, The Salvation Army International Headquarters
Jenty Fairbank, *William and Catherine Booth – God's Soldiers*, Salvationist Publishing and Supplies
Geoffrey Hanks, *God's Special Army*, The Religious Education Press

In this series

S. Tompkins, *Visiting an Anglican Church*, Lutterworth
G. Palmer, *Visiting a Community Church*, Lutterworth
J. Bates, *Visiting a Methodist Church*, Lutterworth
R. Protheroe and R. Meherali, *Visiting a Mosque*, Lutterworth
D. Sullivan, *Visiting a Roman Catholic Church*, Lutterworth
D. K. Babraa, *Visiting a Sikh Temple*, Lutterworth
D. Charing, *Visiting a Synagogue*, Lutterworth

Glossary

Articles of War, a document signed by someone on becoming a Salvation Army soldier at an enrolment, or swearing in, ceremony

Booth, Catherine, William, the founders of The Salvation Army

cadet, a soldier training to be an officer

census board, a group of local officers

citadel, a name for a Salvation Army hall

commanding officer, the leader in charge of a corps

commissioning, a ceremony performed when a person is given a responsible position

company meeting, a Sunday school session when children are taught in small groups

corps, a group of Salvationists in one area

corps cadets, young Salvationists training for Christian activity

dedication, a ceremony in which God's blessing is asked on a child

East London Christian Mission, the group of Christians which became The Salvation Army

General, the international leader of the Army

goodwill, caring work in the community

gospel, the good news of Jesus Christ

guardian, leader of the corps cadets

holiness, purity, godliness

holiness table, a table at the front of a citadel where people may pray for power to be more holy

International Training College, a centre for training Salvation Army officers

Investigation Department, a service for tracing missing relatives

junior soldiers, members of the Army between seven and fourteen years of age

league of mercy, a group of people who work to relieve need in the community

lieutenant, the first rank of a Salvation Army officer – other ranks are captain, major, colonel, commissioner

local officer, a person with a certain responsibility in a corps

mercy seat, a bench in a Salvation Army hall where people kneel to pray (see Exodus 25:21,22)

Musician, The, a weekly Salvation Army newspaper
open fire, begin Salvation Army work in a new area
praise meeting, a service expressing thanks to God
primary, a regular class for children between three and seven
        years of age, led by a primary sergeant
SABAC, Salvation Army Boys' Adventure Corps
Salvationist, a committed member of The Salvation Army
salvation meeting, a religious service which emphasizes the Bible
        teaching about Christ's sacrifice on the cross
sergeant major, a local officer who helps to organize the corps
singing company, a choir of junior soldiers
skeleton army, a group who used force in an attempt to disband
        the Army in the 1880s
testimony, a talk telling of a person's own Christian life
War Cry, The, a weekly Army newspaper
witnessing, identifying as Christians
worship, giving reverant attention to God
young people's band, a brass band composed of junior soldiers
young people's sergeant major, the leader of young people's work
        in the corps
Young Soldier, The, a weekly paper for children produced by the
        Army

Index